SEARCH, SEIZURE AND SURVEY

Issues, Clarifications and Judgements

VED KUMAR JAIN

MANOHAR
2004

First published 2004

ISBN 81-7304-549-6

Published by
Ajay Kumar Jain for
Manohar Publishers & Distributors
4753/23 Ansari Road, Daryaganj
New Delhi 110 002

Printed at
Lordson Publishers Pvt. Ltd.
Delhi 110 007

CONTENTS

1. SEARCH AND SEIZURE

1.1 Introduction

Privacy is a basic human value in the civilized society. Though the Indian Constitution does not explicitly provide for the right to privacy but the Supreme Court has observed it as an essential ingredient of the right to personal liberty under the Constitution. Nothing is more deleterious to a man's physical happiness and health than a calculated interference with his privacy. The right to privacy is implicit in the right to life and liberty guaranteed by Article 21 of the constitution. However, this right is not absolute and cannot be claimed by all individuals in equal measure. There are individuals whose private affairs and behavior may affect their public contact. In such cases the right to know becomes superior countervailing right to deny them the right to privacy. That is why there are provisions under the various acts giving authority to the state to encroach upon the right to privacy of a citizen under certain circumstances. One of the most common instance of such right available across the world is under the Criminal Law. Whenever a person commits any criminal act, it is considered as an offence against the society as it affects the public life. Code of Criminal Procedure, 1973 in India, gives power to the police for search and seizure for various offences committed under the Indian Penal Code.

Taxes are considered as cost of civilization and cost for running the society. Non payment of taxes by a person is considered as an offence against the society as it affects the public life. Accordingly there are provisions under the Income Tax Act giving authority to encroach upon the right to privacy under certain circumstances. These provisions are contained in section 132 of the Income Tax Act, 1961. The procedure prescribed under Code of Criminal Procedure, 1973 relating to searches and seizure applies to search under the Income Tax Act, 1961.

1.2. Circumstances enabling search

Section 132(1) has spelt out three circumstances under which the authorizing authority may issue a warrant of authorization. Under clause (a) action can be taken if a person does not comply with the summons under Section 131(1) or a notice under Section 142(1) of the Act to produce or cause to be produced any books of accounts or other documents. Under clause (b) a formal notice is not essential. In case the authorizing authority has reason to believe that a person, whether or not a notice has been served on him, is not likely to produce books of accounts or other documents, it can issue search warrant. The third clause (c) concerns money, bullion, jewellery or other valuable article or thing representing undisclosed income. In order to invoke clause (c) there must be information with the authorizing authority relating to two matters, firstly, that any person is in possession of money, bullion, jewellery or other valuable article etc. Secondly such money represents either wholly or partly income or property which has not been or would not be disclosed for the purposes of the Act. If the authorizing authority is challenged to prove the basis of his belief he is to prove the same as has been held in the case of Kusum Lata vs CIT (1989)180 ITR 365(Raj). The burden under clause (c) is much stiffer on the authorizing authority to justify the grounds of his belief. For this purpose the authority must have relevant material, on the basis of which he can form an opinion. In the absence of any relevant material the authority would be acting in excess of his power and in violation of the mandatory requirement of Section 132.

It was held by the Supreme Court in the case of ITO vs. Seth Brothers (1969) 74 ITR 836 (SC) that the authority to search has to be based on cogent information on the basis of which the authorized officer has reason to believe that undisclosed income can be detected only on search. The Hon,ble Supreme Court observed as under in the above case:-.

"The section does not confer any arbitrary authority upon the revenue officers. The Commissioner or the Director of Inspection must have, in consequence of information, reason to believe that the statutory conditions for the exercise of the power, to order search, exist. He must record reasons for the belief and he must issue an authorization in favour of a designated officer to search the premises and exercise the powers set out therein. If the officer has reason to believe that any books of account or other documents would be useful for, or relevant to, any proceedings under the Act, he is authorized by law to seize those books of account or other documents, and to place marks of identification therein, to make extracts or copies there from and also to make a note or an inventory of any articles or other things found in the course of the search. Since by the exercise of the power, a serious invasion is made upon the rights, privacy and freedom of the taxpayer, the power must be exercised strictly in accordance with the law and only for the purposes for the which the law authorizes it to be exercised. If the action of the officer issuing the authorization or of the designated officer is challenged the officer concerned must or power under the court about the regularity of his action. If the action is maliciously taken or power under the section is exercised for the collateral purpose, it is liable to be quashed".

Before issue of authorization, authorizing officer specified in section 132(1), must have "reason to believe" that conditions enumerated in cl. (a), (b) or (c) thereof exist and this reason to believe should have been based on "information" in his possession.

"Information" is to be distinguished from "rumour" or "gossip". Rumour is something vague and unverified. Information is something definite and verified. It should not only be authentic but must have rational connection with the requisite belief. In Dr. Nandlal Tahiliani vs. CIT(1988) 170 ITR 592 (Allahabad) the facts that returns were accepted by department and the assessee had never failed to produce documents whenever called upon to produce were not denied. In that context, the fact that the assessee was known for his "roaring practice" and "high rate of fees" was held to be not liable to be construed as constituting "information" in consequence of which the Director could have reason to believe that the assessee had not disclosed his income or would not have disclosed it. It was also observed that living in a posh house was not a material which could result in initiation of proceeding under s.132 of the Act. Special leave petition against this decision was dismissed by the Supreme Court.

In Dr. Nand Lal Tahiliani vs CIT(1988) 170 ITR 592 (Allahabad) Justice Om Prakash has cautioned the department by observing "privacy is a very valuable right of the civilized society and violation thereof is not permissible except by authority of law. Therefore, the department should not only be slow, but slowest in acting upon the information given by an informer. Before acting on the information, source of knowledge of an informer should be fully tested and creditworthiness of the informer also be tested".

The recent decision of Hon'ble Supreme Court in the case of Union of India vs Ajit Jain & Ors.(2003) 260 ITR 80(SC) , upheld the decision of Delhi High Court that a valid search cannot be initiated on the basis of a rumour. In this case the Court held that intimation simpliciter by the CBI that money was found in the possession of the respondent, which according to the CBI was undisclosed, without something more, did not constitute "information" within the meaning of section 132 of the Income Tax Act, 1961, on the basis of which a search warrant could be issued, and the search conducted on the basis of such information and the block assessment made pursuant to such search was not valid and liable to be quashed.

1.3. Ground rules for searches and seizures

(i) Competent Authority

Authorisation for a search can only be ordered by a competent officer after considering the information in his possession provided he has reasons to believe that a search is justified. Before the issue of a search warrant, a formal order is required to be passed by the competent authority.

Information may come from external sources like informers, other government departments or newspapers, magazines and publications. In the case of an informer, it is generally made clear to him that he is liable to be prosecuted under section 182 of the IPC if his allegations are proved false. Internal sources comprise cases developed suo motu on the basis of records, investigation and intelligence gathered by the intelligence wing of the department.

(ii) Objectives of the search.

A search is necessary to secure evidence which is not likely to be made available by issue of summons or by visiting in ordinary course, the premises concerned.. Tax authorities have powers to summon persons and documents. Tax authorities have to resort to search and seizure when there is evidence of undisclosed income or assets which have not been and would not be disclosed in ordinary course.

(iii) Search party

Search party has to be led by an officer. The team must include two respectable witnesses of the locality and technical persons like valuers, etc.

(iv) Examination

Tax authorities thereafter examine the person searched. It is made clear to him that the proceedings are judicial and he is bound to tell the truth. It is also explained to him that the statement is liable to be used against him. This examination is deemed as a judicial proceeding and this statement is admissible as evidence. The purpose of this examination is to secure the explanation of the person regarding the documents and properties before he has an opportunity to concoct an explanation and fabricate evidence. He is not allowed to avail the services of a lawyer at this stage.

(v) **Report to the senior authority**

After the search, the party has to submit a report to the senior authority like Collector, Commissioner, etc. The outcome of search is given to enable the senior officer to judge the *bonafide* of the search and to exercise control over searches carried out.

(vi) **Safeguards**

Section 136(2) of the Customs Act provides for deterrent punishment including imprisonment of the Customs Officer held responsible for vexatious searches. In the cases of Excise and FERA, vexatious searches are punishable by a fine. However there is no such provision under the Income Tax Act, 1961.

(vii) **Arrests**

The power of arrest vests with the Customs, Central Excise and enforcement officers. Income-tax Officers have no powers of arrests. Arrests are generally resorted to in cases where the detected offence is of a serious nature and the case appears to be fit for criminal prosecution. Persons are generally not arrested when the intention is only to have departmental proceedings. Persons are arrested when there is a gravity of offence. evidence of personal culpability, a strong *prima facie* case and likelihood of person tampering with the evidence by remaining at large or absconding.

Books of account and documents seized cannot be retained for more than 30 days from the date of assessment order under section 153A or 158BC except for recorded reasons and with the approval of the Chief Commissioner, Commissioner, Director General or Director. Law specifically provides that the person concerned may make copies of the documents concerned.

(viii) **Rights of the person searched:**

(i) To see the warrant of authorization duly signed and sealed by the issuing authority.

(ii) To verify the identity of each member of the search party.

(iii) To make personal search of all members of the search party before the start of the search and on conclusion of the search.

(iv) To insist on personal search of ladies being taken only by a lady, with strict regard to decency.

(v) To have at least two respectable and independent residents of the locality as witnesses.

(vi) A lady occupying an apartment being searched has a right to withdraw before the search party enters, if according to custom, she does not appear in public.

(vii) To call a medical practitioner in case of emergency.

(viii) To allow the children to go to school, after checking their bags.

(ix) To have the facility of having meals, etc., at the normal time.

(x) To inspect the seals placed on various receptacles, sealed in course of search and subsequently at the time of reopening of the seals.

(xi) Every person who is examined under section 132(4) has a right to ensure that the facts so stated by him have been recorded correctly.

(xii) To have a copy of the *panchanama* together with all the annexures.

(xiii) To have a copy of any statement that is used against him by the Department.

(xiv) To have inspection of the seized books of account, etc., or to take extracts therefrom in the presence of any of the authorized officers or any other person empowered by him.

(xv) To make an application objecting to the approval given by the Commissioner of Income-tax for retention of books and documents beyond 180 days from the date of the seizure.

(ix) **Duties of the person searched:**

(i) To allow free and unhindered ingress into the premises.

(ii) To see the warrant of authorization and put signature on the same.

(iii) To identify all receptacles in which assets or books of account and documents are kept and to hand over keys to such receptacles to the authorized officer.

(iv) To identify' and explain the ownership of the assets, books of account and documents found in the premises.

(v) To identify every individual in the premises and to explain their relationship to the person being searched. He should not mislead by personation. If he cheats by pretending to be some other person or knowingly substitutes one person for another, it is an offence punishable under section 416 of the Indian Penal Code.

(vi) Not to allow or encourage the entry of any unauthorized person into the premises.

(vii) Not to remove any article from its place without notice or knowledge of the authorized officer. If he secrets or destroys any document with the intention of preventing the same from being produced or used as evidence before the Court or public servant, he shall be punishable with imprisonment or fine or both, in accordance with section 204 of the Indian Penal Code.

(viii) To answer all queries truthfully and to the best of his knowledge. He should not allow any third party to either interfere or prompt while his statement is being recorded by the authorized officer. In doing so, he should keep in mind that—

(a)If he refuses to answer a question on a subject relevant to the search operation, he shall be punishable with imprisonment or fine or both, under section 179 of the Indian Penal Code.

(b)Being legally bound by an oath or affirmation to state the truth, if he makes a false statement, he shall be punishable with imprisonment or fine or both under section 181 of the Indian Penal Code.

(c)Similarly, if he provides evidence which is false and which he knows or believes to be false, he is liable to be punished under section 191 of the Indian Penal Code.

(ix) To affix his signature on the recorded statement, inventories and the *panchanama.*

(x) To ensure that peace is maintained throughout the duration of the search, and to cooperate with the search party in all respects so that the search action is concluded at the earliest and in a peaceful manner.

(xi) Similar co-operation should be extended even after the search action is over, so as to enable the authorized officer to complete necessary follow-up investigations at the earliest.

(x) **Guidelines for seizure of jewellery and ornaments in course of search.**

(i) In the case of a wealth-tax assessee, gold jewellery and ornaments found in excess of the gross weight declared in the wealth-tax return only need be seized.

(ii) In the case of a person not assessed to wealth-tax, gold jewellery and ornaments to the extent of 500 gms. per married lady, 250 gms. per unmarried lady and 100 gms. per male member of the family, need not be seized.

(iii) The authorized officer may, having regard to the status of the family and the custom and practices of the community to which the family belongs and other circumstances of the case, decide to exclude a larger quantity of jewellery and ornaments from seizure. This should be reported to the Director of Income-tax/Commissioner authorizing the search at the time of furnishing the search report.

(iv) In all cases, a detailed inventory of the jewellery and ornaments found must be prepared to be used for assessment purposes.

[Instruction No. 1916, dated 11th May, 1994: (1994) 120 Taxation (St.) 98].

(xi) **Criminal Procedure Code provisions relating to searches.**

Chapter VII of Criminal Procedure Code, 1973, deals with searches and allied matters. Under section 91, a court may summon a document or thing. Section 93(1) provides for the issue of a search warrant if the court has reason to believe that the person concerned, in spite of summons, will not produce the document or thing. Section 93(2) empowers the court to restrict a search warrant in the manner thought fit. Section 94 provides for empowering, by the court concerned, of a police officer above the rank of a constable, to enter and search a place and to take possession of the document, thing or property, which is the subject-matter. Section 165 (Chapter XII) provides that the police officer, although not empowered under a search warrant, on his having reasonable grounds for believing that anything necessary for the purposes of the investigation may be found in any place, may, after recording in writing the grounds of his belief and specifying in such writing, so far as is possible, the thing for which the search is to be made, enter the place and search, or cause a search to be made, for such a thing in any (such) place.

Section 100(4) lays down that the search has to be made in the presence of two or more independent and respectable witnesses who are inhabitants of the locality. For that purpose, the searching officer has to make a *panchanama.* Section 100(5) provides that a list of all things seized and of the place in which they are respectively found shall be prepared and signed also by such witnesses.

Interpreting the provisions of Section 100(4) of the Criminal Procedure Code, 1973, which requires that before making a search, the officer or other person about to make it, shall call upon two or more independent and respectable inhabitants of the locality in which the place to be searched is situated, in *Pradeep Narayan Madgaonkar vs. State of Maharashtra* [(1995) 4 SCC 255, 261], it has been held, on facts, that the Court cannot lose sight of the fact that these police officials did not join any *independent* witnesses of the *locality* and made an attempt to create an impression on the courts that both witnesses were -*witnesses of locality and were independent,* knowing fully well that one was a witness who was under their influence and 'available' to them, as he had been joining the raids earlier also and the other was a close associate of the first, their friendship having developed during the days of gambling when admittedly the police never conducted any raid at their gambling den. The very fact that the police officers joined these two witnesses in the raid creates a doubt about the fairness of the investigation.

(xii) **Provisions of the Criminal Procedure Code, how far applicable.**

By Section 132(13) of the Income Tax Act 1961, the provisions of the Code of Criminal Procedure, 1973, relating to searches and seizure have been made applicable, so far as may be, to searches made under section 132 of the Act. The reference to code of criminal procedure is for limited purpose i.e. the officers concerned shall issue the necessary warrant, keep present at least two independent and respectable persons of the locality to witness search, and generally carry out the search in the manner provided by the Code of Criminal Procedure. But section 132(13) does not imply that the limitations prescribed by section 165 of the Code of Criminal Procedure are also incorporated therein and go to empower an income tax authority to carry out a search without having been properly authorized under a regular warrant [ITO v. Seth Bros., (1969) 74 ITR 836, 844(SC)].

In order to give full meaning to the expression *so far as may be' in section 132(13), that sub section should be interpreted to mean that, broadly, the procedure relating to search as enacted in section 165 of the Criminal Procedure Code shall be followed. But if a deviation becomes necessary to carry out the purposes of the Income Tax Act, it would be permissible except that when challenged before a court of law, justification will have to be offered for the deviation *[Dr. Partap Singh v. Director of Enforcement,* (1985)155 ITR 166, 174 (SC)]. Also see, *Bishnu Krishna Shrestha v. Union of India,* (1987) 168 ITR 815, 841 - 42 (Cal), *Virendra Kumar Goela v. State of West Bengal,* (1994) 94 STC 266, 286 - 87 (WBTT)

1.4. Evidentiary value of documents found during the course of search

As is usual, various books of accounts documents are found and sized during the course of search. As per section 132(4A) there is presumption that such books of accounts documents, belongs to such person from whose possession or control there are found. Further there is presumption that the contents of such books of accounts and other documents are true and that the signature and every other part of such books of accounts and other documents are true and that the signature and every other part of such books of accounts and other documents which purports to be in the handwriting of any particular person or which may reasonably be assumed to be in the handwriting of any particular person are in that person's handwriting.

It is to be noted that the presumption is only with regard to the person from whose possession and control the books of accounts and documents are found. Moreover this presumption is rebuttable presumption. Important judgments on this issue including those on loose papers found in search have been discussed in the chapter 'Important Judgments'..

1.5. Stock in trade not to be seized during search

A provision has been inserted by the Finance Act,2003 to provide that stock-in- trade including that of bullion, jewellery or other valuable article or thing found as a result of search shall not be seized. However, the authorized officer shall be entitled to make an inventory of such stock in trade of the business. The above-said provision is applicable with effect from 1st June, 2003.

1.6. Release of seized assets

The Finance Act, 2002 had introduced a provision authorizing the Assessing Officer to release the seized assets with the approval of the Chief Commissioner or Commissioner where the nature and source of acquisition of seized assets is explained to the satisfaction of the AO after applying such assets first towards the existing liability. Such release of assets is to be done within a period of 120 days from the date on which the last of the authorizations for search was executed. In order to provide sufficient time to the AO to decide the application of the assessee for release of seized assets, it has been provided that application for release of assets be made within a period of 30 days from the end of the month in which the asset was seized. The assessee is required to be alert and make application explaining the nature and source of acquisition of seized assets immediately after the seizure of such assets.

The above provision of release of seized assets however does not take into account the ground realitics. The application is to be made to the AO within 30 days and release order is to be passed within 120 days. During this period, the AO is not even aware about the search. He can decide the issue only after receipt of appraisal report which usually comes very late. The power to release assets ideally, should have been given, both to the authorized officer and the AO. The limitation of 120 days should be on the authorized officer and there should be no limitation period prescribed for the AO.

1.7. Interest on seized money

As per the provision of section 132B assessee is entitled to interest at the rate of 8 per cent (reduced to 6 per cent with effect from 8th September, 2003) on the amount of money seized as reduced by the amount of money if any released under the proviso to section 132B and of the proceeds of the assets sold in excess of the existing tax liabilities and the liabilities on completion of the block assessment including penalty and interest. However the interest shall be payable from the expiry of the period of 120 days from the execution of the last of the authorizations for search and till the date of completion of block assessment. It is not understood why interest should start after 120 days and why not from the date of seizure or realization of sale proceeds, as the money collected get deposited in the bank account on the very next day of the seizure.

1.8. No confession or forced surrender of income at the time of search or survey

The Finance Minister had made a statement in the Parliament that no forced surrender will be obtained at the time of search or survey. The CBDT has issued circular dt 10th March, 2003 whereby it has been clarified that no confessional statement for surrender of additional income will be forcibly obtained at the time of search and survey. Text of circular is given in the Appendix – I.

1.9. New procedure introduced for search cases

The block assessment procedure introduced in 1995 and in operation for the last 8 years with various amendments from time to time has been abolished in respect of search carried out after 31st May, 2003. In place of the block assessment a new scheme of reassessment has been introduced by inserting three new sections, 153A, 153B and 153C of the Income Tax Act for assessment in the case of search. As per these new provisions, the AO is required to issue notice in respect of 6 assessment years preceding the assessment year relevant to the previous year in which search is conducted asking the assessee to file return of income. Thereafter the AO shall assess or reassess the total income of these 6 assessment years. The assessment or reassessment pending in respect of any assessment year as on the date of initiation of search shall abate. The time limit for completion of assessment is a period of 2 years from the end of the financial year in which the last of the authorizations for search is executed. However, the period during which the assessment proceeding is stayed or the time required for obtaining an audit report under Section 142(2A), the time provided to give an opportunity of rehearing on the change of the officer and the time during which the application of settlement is pending for admission is to be excluded while computing the limitation. A provision similar on the line of Section 158BD has been inserted for making assessment of income of a person where the AO is satisfied that the assets found or the books of accounts or other documents seized belong to such other person. However, the period of limitation in such cases shall also be 2 years from the end of the financial year in which last of the authorizations for the search was executed as against the present provisions of Section 158 BE which provide a period of 2 years from the end of the month in which the notice under Section 158BD is served on such other person.

The rate of tax under this new scheme shall be the normal tax rate applicable on the income of the assessee for each of the assessment years as against the flat rate of 60 per cent under block assessment. However, the assessee will be liable to pay interest and penalty as per the regular provisions of the Act and will not have the benefit available under the block assessment scheme of not levying penalty to the extent of the income disclosed in the block return. The new scheme of reassessment has raised following issues which need to be addressed:-

(i) Section 153A does not mention any time limit for issue of notice by the AO. In case notice is issued at the end of the limitation period, it can place tremendous pressure on taxpayers to furnish six years' returns.

(ii) Clause(a) to Section 153 A does not spell out any time limit which should be given in the notice requiring submission of return in response to notice issued under section 153(A) for six years preceding the previous year in which the search takes place. This may be used in an arbitrary manner by the Assessing Officer concerned who may chose to give the time of his liking, may be one week, or one month or two months etc. If we recollect the minimum time that was to be given under section 158 BC was 15 days and maximum time was 45 days within which the return for the block period was required to be filed.

(iii) It is nowhere stated that Section 153 A would override the provisions of Section 143(3), therefore it is a moot point as to whether the findings of regular assessment would remain intact in the said assessment or not. In an hypothetical case if an Assessing Officer chooses to assess a particular component of income in a manner different from the one earlier done in assessment under section 143(3) as to whether this would lead to further litigation or not.

(iv) As per the ratio of decisions of various courts and now settled law, a mere change of opinion does not empower the Assessing Officer to proceed with the re-assessment under section 147. Therefore, it is unclear as to how the Assessing Officer while drafting an assessment under section 153 A could change an opinion with respect to allowability of expenditures and losses.

(v) It is again judicially well settled that in reassessment, assessee cannot be permitted to raise new claim for deduction not earlier raised during the course of regular assessment. Therefore, it is unclear as to whether the assessee would be able to raise the claim for deduction for the first time in a search assessment.

(vi) It is inexplicable that in a case where no incriminating document or material is found in respect of any of the years contained in the six years preceding the previous year in which the search took place, the assessee has to suffer the harassment of having to get his case again assessed under section 153A consequent to a search. It is also contrary to the judgment of Hon'ble Supreme Court contained in 106 ITR 1 in the case of Parasuram Pottery Works Co .Ltd. vs .ITO., wherein the Hon'ble Supreme Court has held that there must be a point of finality in all legal proceedings whereas provisions of section 153A seem to completely bypass this fundamental policy of law.

(vii) The search may show that the concealment or inaccurate furnishing of particulars, relate only to one or two years. Why then should the returns be filed for six years – even for the years for which assessments have already been completed and no concealment is relatable to those years? Prior to the insertion of the block assessment scheme, the concealed incomes were assessed or reassessed in the years to which these belonged by reopening of only those assessments under section 148 of the Act.

(viii) Sections 148 contain inbuilt safeguards in the matter of reopening of the completed assessments, on the existence of 'reason to believe and recording of reasons before issue of notice under section 148. There is no such requirement under the new scheme. Once a search is there, there will be re-assessment for six years irrespective of the fact whether adverse material belong to all the six years or to any one or more years of assessment.

(ix) The block assessment scheme was introduced to solve the issue of allocation of concealed income to different years. No solution has been found to this problem under the new scheme. There will be protracted litigation on the issue whether the income pertains to a particular year or not. Ultimately the assessee may have the benefit of getting the addition knocked off technically on the ground that income does not pertain to a particular year.

(x) Section 153C penalizes persons other than those searched merely because their valuables are found at the place of the person searched, without there being any indication of these being undisclosed. This is contrary to Section 158BD of block assessment which provided for making block assessment to the AO only when the AO having jurisdiction over the assessee searched "is satisfied that any undisclosed income belongs to that person".

Now if a person keeps his valuables (whether explained or unexplained) with another person even for safe custody, he would be subjected to the reassessment of six years.

xi) Under the new scheme assessment for all six years shall become time barred on 31st March. In the case of a search, usually there are number of assesses in the group. Moreover cases of search are usually transferred to Central Circle. This will now create administrative difficulties as an AO will now have a number of group cases getting time barred on 31st March and he will be required to write six asstt order for each case.

The new scheme in place of the old scheme has been introduced on the ground that the block assessment scheme has failed in its objective of early resolution of such assessment and has spawned a fresh scheme of litigation. However, the fact remains that the provisions of the block assessment procedure had settled by and large by the judgements of various courts and the new scheme of reassessment will create its own new issues for litigation and will take its own time before being settled by the courts. Further the flat rate of 60 per cent had inbuilt element of about 100 per cent penalty for concealment on the income disclosed voluntarily by the assessee in the block return. Under the new proposed scheme, the tax rate applicable being normal rate, the assessee will have a better option to get the dispute settled through the Settlement Commission and pay tax at the normal rate as against the flat rate of 60 per cent presently payable even while settling the dispute of block assessment through Settlement Commission. No doubt the provisions of tax compliance should be stringent. However, taking into consideration the ground realities, voluntary compliance at every stage should be encouraged. The procedure of block assessment was introduced only with this objective. By closing the option of voluntary compliance in search cases at higher cost, the defaulting taxpayers will be compelled to opt for litigation for the income, which he had otherwise readily agreed to offer for taxation. In this process he may or may not succeed but can definitely prolong the litigation. The block asstt scheme introduced and accepted by the government and being in operation for quite a number of years should not have been discarded simply because there is a change in the perception of the present day policy makers. A well thought out scheme introduced in the past even if it had to be discarded, the same should have been done after thorough debate by including economists, tax experts, representatives from trade and industry. The time and energy put in by the tax officers, tax experts and the judges in understanding and implementing the block assessment scheme has gone down the drain in one go.

2. SURVEY

2.1. Introduction

Survey under the Income-tax Act is regulated by section 133A. This section was inserted by the Finance Act, 1964, with effect from 1st April, 1964; thereafter the scope of the section was radically enlarged substituting it by the Taxation Laws (Amendment) Act, 1975, with effect from 1st October, 1975 to present one.

Survey under the above section can be conducted on an assessees who do not pay income-tax and also on assessees whom, the officials suspect, have more income than was declared in his returns.

The term 'survey' has not been defined under the Act but as per the Oxford Dictionary the same has been meant as "to take a general view of; examine the general condition of'.

Search and seizure commonly knows as raid can be performed at any time in the 24 hours of a day of the places mentioned in the warrant of authorization belonging to the intended person, under section 132 of the Act and has very large scope while the timings, places and scope of survey are restricted under section 133A. *If, as* a result of a survey, any information comes out on which the authorities empowered to authorize search have reason to believe that any of the conditions laid down in clauses (a), (b) or (c) of sub-section (1) of section 132 of the Act has been fulfilled, then search can follow the survey.

2.2. Place of Survey

An Income-tax authority acting under section 133A can survey the place at which business or profession of a person is carried on, whether such place be the principal place of such business or profession or not, i.e, it may be the branch office or godown. Authority cannot enter residential place of the person; in other words, he cannot survey the place belonging to person where his business or profession related activities are not carried on. Further, if a person is conducting business or profession from his residence, only that portion of residence, from where the business or profession is conducted, has to be surveyed. However, where the person states that any of his books of account or other documents or any part of his cash or stock or other valuable article or thing relating to his business or profession are kept, at a place other than where business/profession is carried on then such place will come under the ambit of survey. For this purpose, the place may be the residential place of the person or the office or residence of his advocate or chartered accountant, or any other place etc. as stated.

2.3. Timings of survey

An Income-tax authority acting under sub-section (1) of section 133A can enter any place of business or profession only during the normal working hours for conducting such business or profession of the person. If it happens to be holiday or the weekly rest or it is closed for some other reason, then it cannot be forcibly opened for the purpose of survey. When the survey process starts within the working hours, then it may continue and last even after the close of the business hours or after sunset.

2.4. Survey in connection with expenditure at a function, ceremony

Under Section 133A(5) of the Act, the tax authorities have power to obtain information in respect of the expenditure incurred at a function or ceremony. The power is limited to obtain information and record statements. It is to be noted that such power can be exercised only after such function, ceremony or event not during the course of such function, ceremony.

2.5. Facility to Income-tax authorities

Sub-section (4) of section 133A debars an Income-tax authority during the course of survey from removing any cash, stock or other valuable article or thing but in terms of sub-section (3) of section 133A such authority can put identification marks or take extracts or copies from books of account and also may prepare an inventory of cash, stock or other valuable article or thing checked or verified by him.

Under sub-section (6) of section 133A, a person whose premises are surveyed is required to cooperate with the Income-tax authority in respect of affording him facility to inspect books of account, checking and verifying of cash, stock position, providing any information or recording of statement; otherwise, if he evades or refused to co-operate, Income-tax authority shall have powers under sub-section (1) of section 131, which includes the power to examine a person on oath and compelling him for the production of books of account and other documents. for enforcing compliance of the requirements of section 133A.

2.6. Power of survey—A piece of unguarded administrative power

As per the settled principle of the administrative law, the conferment of power on an administrative authority without reasonable and effective safeguarded is neither permissible nor sustainable. Effective control and safeguard are required to be embodied just to check any sort of misuse of such a power by the authority concerned.

As a matter of fact, keeping in view the said fundamental requirement, the statute does let the power and safeguard to do side-by-side. The obvious illustration, to substantiate the point are the phrases "reason to believe", "reasons to be recorded in writing" and "with the prior approval of (some higher authority)", which are the common feature of every such provision which purports to confer any power or jurisdiction on any tax-official. For instance, an Assessing Officer may initiate the reassessment proceedings under section 147 only if he has reason to believe that an otherwise taxable income has escaped assessment due to any of the specified reasons. However, in sharp contrast to the aforestated general statutory trend, section 133A nowhere stipulates any sort of control or check. An authorized officer may conduct the survey capriciously or just to harass the person concerned.

2.7. An uncontrolled administrative power must be shorn-off by the Court—Landmark ruling of the Calcutta High Court in Dr.Vijay Pahwa's case

The adverse remarks made by the Calcutta High Court in the recent case of Dr. Vijay Pahwa (2001)250 ITR 354(Cal) viz., 'The Income-tax Officers and authorities do not have any power to interrupt the ordinary peaceful citizens of the country in any manner they like by utilizing the large powers given to them, without keeping strictly within the four comers of those large powers. Since the powers vested are large, even a millimeter of departure there- from must be immediately shorn-off by the impartial Courts of Law if the country is to continue to remain a free one", simply shows the judicial resentment over the misuse of large powers conferred on the tax-officials by the Income-tax Act.

The relevant facts of the instant case are, in fact, very shocking as despite the up to date completed assessments of the petitioner-assessee, on 17th April, 1995, certain Income-tax authorities visited the-chamber of the petitioner-assessee, purporting to conduct a survey under section 133A of the Act. What is more, on the same day, that is, 17th April, 1995, summon was issued for the production of books which was executed on the same day and that too within 30 minutes. All the books of the petitioner-assessee reached the Income-tax Office. Immediately thereafter those books were impounded at the office of the Income-tax authorities. Interestingly. all this happened on 17th April, 1995. Thereupon, the assessee challenged the validity of survey by way of a writ before the Calcutta High Court. The learned Single Judge, who heard the petition, having found that the Deputy Commissioner of Income-tax, who led the survey, had blatantly misused the survey jurisdiction by adopting illegal procedure (in the matter of issuing summons) and high-handed actions, made him (the Deputy Commissioner of Income-tax, the leader of the survey party) personally liable to pay one day's costs to the writ petitioner, assessed at Rs. 35,000 by way of interim order irrespective of final result of the writ petition. The costs have been ordered to be paid within a fortnight from the date of the passing of the order and in case of default in the payment of costs, choice has been given to the petitioner to recover the same even by instituting a contempt proceeding before the Court. The finding of the learned Single Judge in the afore discussed case has surprisingly multifarious dimension. The finding, in the first place, may be said to be a first ever judicial attempt to make the tax-officials accountable for their wrongful acts. Secondly, although the Court has made the leader of the survey party personally liable to compensate the petitioner but the question is, does such an award hold ground, especially in view of the specific immunity granted by section 293 of the Act to all the Government's officers. Thirdly, it is not clear, whether the Central Government could be made liable on the footing of 'vicarious liability'.

2.8. Do's and Don'ts of the tax authorities during survey

On analytical study of the relevant provisions it emerges that following are the powers conferred on the tax authorities:

(i) To enter the business premises, during business hours, after disclosing identity;

(ii) To disclose the purpose and to commence survey of the business premises, without disturbing the ongoing business and without dislocating the normal business;

(iii) To call for the books of accounts and other documents as may be available; as may be required for the purpose of the survey; to inspect such books of accounts or other documents; to put identification marks and to take copies of such documents or papers as may be necessary for the purpose of the Act, to prepare an inventory of the cash to check and verify the same with the books of accounts and documents. As per the amendment carried out by the Finance Act 2002, to impound and retain in the custody, books of accounts and other documents inspected, if need be.

(iv) To prepare an inventory of the stock and other valuable article or thing which may be found and to check and verify the same from the books of accounts and documents;

(v) To seek clarifications on aspects of discrepancy as also to solicit such information as may be required and which may be useful for or relevant to any proceeding under the Act;

(vi) To provide copy of inventories of cash, stock, other valuable article or thing, books of accounts and documents found in the course of survey;

(vii) To do any other act in support of the above said aspects and after completion of survey to leave business place, peacefully and without causing any harassment or giving any threats or causing any fear;

The tax authorities are not empowered to do the following acts:

(i) To remove, take in possession, or seize, cash, stock-in-trade and other valuable article or thing, etc., found in the course of the survey.

(ii) Not to pressurize the taxpayer to surrender any specific amount and to give any assurance as to non-liability for interest, tax, penalty, etc;

(iii) Not to issue any summon under section 131(1) of the Act without recording reasons therefore and not to impound the produced books of accounts or documents without recording reasons, and not to retain for more than 10 days without seeking prior approval of the higher authority and without communicating reasons as well as the approval;

(iv) Not to do any act against intent purpose and objectives of the law and contrary to the provisions of law; and

(v) Not to have any bias, malafide.

2.9. Rights and obligations of an assessee.

Following are the duties and obligations of an assessee under survey:

(i) To permit entry to the officers after satisfying their identity;

(ii) To afford facility to the Income-tax authority to conduct survey, to co-operate during survey and to maintain peaceful atmosphere;

(iii) To assist in preparing inventory of books of accounts or documents or cash or stock-in-trade or any other article or thing which may be found in the course of survey and to see that such inventories are detailed, exhaustive and authentic; to furnish requisite clarifications;

(iv) To give statements truthfully and completely, avoiding falsity or incorrectness;

(v) To put signatures on the inventories and statements after carefully reading, vouching its correctness and obtaining its copies;

(vi) To extend facility so as to complete the survey as expeditiously as possible;

(vii) To truthfully disclose all the material facts and to be guided by the sound advice of his tax consultant;

(viii) To do any other act or step or take steps which may be deemed desirable by the tax consultant, on the facts and in totality of the circumstances.

2.10. Seeking of assistance of tax consultants

Law does not permit an assessee to insist the tax authorities not to conduct survey till arrival of the tax consultant irrespective whether he is an advocate or a chartered accountant or a tax practitioner. However, an assessee may request and if permitted may call for, to assist in proper conduct of the survey. Section 288(1) of the Act provides that any assessee, who is entitled or required to attend before any Income-tax authority or the Appellate Tribunal in connection with any proceeding under the Act, otherwise than when required under section 131 to attend personally for examination on oath or affirmation, may subject to the other provisions of section 288 attend by an authorized representative. The said section does not entitle an authorized representative to attend the survey proceedings. Section 30 of the Advocates Act, 1961 entitles every advocate, whose name is entered in the State roll, as of right, to practice throughout the territories of India in all

Courts including the Supreme Court, before any Tribunal or person legally authorized to take evidence and before any other authority or person before whom such advocate is by or under any law for the time being in force entitled to practice.

The said section also does not help in seeking personal presence in survey proceedings.

The Supreme Court in the case of Pool Pandi vs Supdt. Central Excise (1992) 75 Comp. Cas. 504 (SC) did not approve the view that assessees are entitled to presence of their lawyers when they are questioned during the investigation under the provisions of the Customs Act and Foreign Exchange Regulation Act. Same is the view during survey, search and similar proceedings under the Act.

If the books of accounts and documents of an assessee are not found at his business premises but are lying with his Chartered Accountant or Advocate or Tax Consultant or Accountant or any other person, the tax authority shall be within its rights to reach such place and conduct survey.

2.11. Use of material found in survey

The Income-tax authority shall be entitled to use the material found in the course of the survey while making assessment for the relevant assessment year(s). However, the tax authorities are required to confront the material so found and to seek comments and explanation thereon. The taxpayer shall be entitled to explain the discrepancies noticed by the tax authorities.

.It is advisable to take survey seriously, to examine the material found and to compute income for the year under survey in respect of excess stock-in-trade, unaccounted cash, valuable article or thing or such transactions which are not correctly recorded.

If the income relating to the previous year, is disclosed in the return to be filed after the survey, liability shall be only in respect of tax and no penalty shall be leviable under section 271(l)(c) of the Act. Payment of interest can be avoided by payment of advance tax and furnishing of return by the specified date. It is to be noted that penalty for concealment of income under section 271(1)(c) is leviable only when there is concealment of particulars of income or furnishing of inaccurate particulars of such income. Explanation 5 to section 271(1)(c) extends the scope of concealment in the case of search. As per this explanation when in the course of search under section 132, the assessee is found to be the owner of any money, bullion, jewellery or other valuable article or thing which does not represent the income or the transactions resulting in such income recorded in the books of accounts, before the date of search, then such money, bullion etc is deemed to be concealed income. This explanation is applicable in the case of search under section 132 only and not to survey carried out under section 133A of the Act. Accordingly any excess stock, cash etc found during the course of survey, if it pertains to current year and of the year for which the return has not fallen due, then no penalty for concealment can be levied. If any document or paper or transaction relate to the assessment years, for which returns have been filed before the survey, but detected after the survey, it is advisable to file revised/supplementary returns forthwith, after making payment of tax and interest. Penalty in such instances may be leviable in law but can be avoided on co-operation and voluntary payment of taxes. It is trite, the year of taxation can not be changed. Tax shall be leviable for the year during which detected income was earned, accrued or arose. Other consequences shall follow. Sometimes the Income-tax authority desire to pay by way of advance tax in respect of income of earlier years, which is erroneous and not in conformity with law. By doing so payment by way of advance tax shall be in excess and one shall be incurring liability for payment of tax interest and penalty for those years.

Income which is detected in the course of the survey, deserve to be recorded in the regular books of accounts, so as to bring in the normal channel. In case of excess stock-in-trade or unaccounted for or unexplained cash, valuable article or thing, etc., its value should be brought in the books by debit to the respective account and credit to the profit and loss account and capital account as the case may be. Sometimes, it happens that stock-in-trade is in short and cash-in-hand is found in excess. In such circumstances, it can be claimed that cash-in-hand is sale consideration of the stock-in-trade found in short and therefore, it should be telescoped and there should not be double addition, one for excess unexplained cash-in-hand and another for shortage of stock-in-trade.

2.12. Amendments made by Finance Act, 2003

(i) Survey only after prior approval of Joint Director or Joint Commissioner.

A new provision has been inserted with effect from 1st June, 2003 to provide that no survey shall be conducted without obtaining the approval of the Joint Director or the Joint Commissioner of Income Tax.

(ii) Retention period of books of accounts impounded has been reduced to 10 days

The Finance Act, 2002 had introduced a new clause empowering the income tax authorities to impound and retain the books of accounts or other documents inspected by the authorized officer after recording the reason for doing so. The period of retention of such books of accounts and documents was limited to 15 days. The same has been reduced to 10 days with effect from 1at June, 2003. However, this period can be extended with the approval of the Chief Commissioner or Director-General.

(iii) Income tax authority for the purpose of survey to include Tax Recovery Officer

Definition of income tax authority for the purpose of carrying out survey under Section 133A of the Income Tax Act has been amended to include Tax Recovery Officer. This amendment has empowered the Tax Recovery Officer to carry out survey and may be invoked, where recovery is pending and this can be a cause of undue harassment to the taxpayer. The existing provisions of recovery were more than sufficient, if appropriately invoked by the Tax Recovery Officer.

3. IMPORTANT JUDGEMENTS

A. Undisclosed Income

3.1. The concept of undisclosed income is akin to the concept of concealed income and therefore AO must bring positive material on record to prove falsity in the books of accounts. The entries recorded in the books of accounts can not be rejected in a light hearted manner on mere suspicion and surmises however grave. Kasat Paper and Pulp Ltd vs ACIT 74 ITD 455 (Pune) Page 466, para 11,

3.2. Income on the basis of regular book of accounts and other documents even though seized can not form part of undisclosed income. 75 ITD 103 (Nag) (Rainbow Distillaries (P) Ltd vs DCIT) at page 114, para 17.

3.3. As per clause (d) of section 158BB(1) entries relating to such income or transactions as recorded in the books of accounts and other documents maintained in the normal course on or before the date of search are to be excluded while computing undisclosed income. Without any allegation that these books in which these entries appear are not regular books of accounts, amounts as reflected in regular books of accounts can by no stretch of imagination be subject matter of undisclosed income under chapter XIV-B. Kasat Paper & Pulp Ltd, 74 ITD 455(Nag).

3.4. Transactions which are part of the regular return filed by the assessee can not be subject matter of 158BA for computing undisclosed income as held by Delhi High Court in the case of CIT vs Ravi Kant Jain (2001)250 ITR 141(Del).

3.5. As per clause (d) of section 158BB(1), books of accounts and other documents maintained in the normal course of business can not be subject matter of undisclosed income as held in the case of Control Touch Electronics (Pune) Pvt. Ltd vs ACIT 72 TTJ (Pune) 65, relevant observations on page 71 para 9.

3.6. In the case of J.K. Narayanan (HUF) vs ACIT 242 ITR 45 (AT) Mad, it has been held that no addition can be made on the basis of information contained in the return. The income declared in the return cannot be called undisclosed income and in the absence of undisclosed income no addition can be sustained.

3.7. Not disclosed income must mean income which is liable to be taxed but which has not been disclosed. Page 48 of 194 ITR LR Gupta vs UOI 194 ITR 32 (Del).

3.8. Onus is upon AO to establish that an entry in the books of account or other document represents concealed income. 45 ITD 12 (Bangalore)

3.9. Where existence of transaction is already known to the deptt. it will not fall within the definition of undisclosed income (1992) 194 ITR 32 (Del).

3.10. What is disclosed cannot be undisclosed. LR Gupta's case (1992) 194 ITR 32 (Del).

3.11. No roving enquiry in respect of completed assessment. Indore Construction (P) Ltd. (1999) 71 ITD 128(Ind).

3.12. Provisions of Chapter XIV-B has to be construed strictly and scope can not be extended so as to permit re-examination. 72 ITD 128 Hyd (Essem Intra Port Services (P)Ltd.

3.13. Return to be adjudicated with reference to material obtained during search operation proceedings. Assessing Officer not conferred with power to make estimate of income *de hors* material in his possession. A.O. is justified in resorting to best judgement assessment only if returns are not in accordance with the material on record.

3.14. An expenditure such as commission recorded in the books of account can not be, by any stretch of imagination, called as an undisclosed income. Rainbow Distillaries vs DCIT 75 ITD 103 (Nagpur).

3.15. If prior to the date of the search, the assessee has disclosed the particulars of income either in the return or in the course of assessment proceedings to the A.O. or where the return has not become due, the same are duly recorded in the regular books of account then such income can not be treated as undisclosed income. Parekh Foods Ltd vs DCIT 64 Ltd 396 (Pune).

3.16. Definition of undisclosed income would include any entries in the books of account or other document showing concealment of real sources of income. The requirement of Section 158BD is only *prima facie* satisfaction of the Assessing Officer that in search operation there is material to show undisclosed income of person other than one who is searched. There is no merit in the contention that action under section 158BD can not be taken against another person unless books of account or other document of such other person are found. Rushil Industries Ltd vs Harsha Prakash 251 ITR 608 (Gujarat)

B. **Income**

3.17. The SC in the case of Parimisetti Seetharamma vs CIT 57 ITR 532 (SC) held that burden is on revenue to prove that particular receipt is taxable. Every receipt is not income.

3.18. It is revenue's onus before assessing any receipts as taxable income and this can be proved or established only on the basis of some material. ACIT vs Shailesh S. Shah 59 TTJ 574 (Mum).

3.19. Revenue can tax only those receipts which first have been proved to be income in the hands of recipient. Mehboob Productions (P) Ltd vs CIT 106 ITR 758 (Bom).

C. **Suspicion**

3.20. Suspicion howsoever strong can not take part of proof 37 ITR 271 (SC) Uma Charan Shaw vs CIT 37 ITR 271

3.21. Mere doubt is not enough. The AO must bring positive material on record to prove the falsity. Kasat Paper & Pulp Ltd vs ACIT Pune 74 ITD 455 Pune , page 466, para 11.

3.22. In the case of Charan Singh vs State of UP ATR 1976 SC 520, the SC has observed that the Court must guard against the danger of allowing conjecture or suspicion to take place of legal proof. If two views are possible on any evidence, one proving guilt, another proving innocence, the view favourable to the accused be adopted. Harendra Narain Singh vs State of Bihar, 1991 SC 184 at page 184

3.23. CIT vs Daulat Ram Rawatmull 87 ITR 349 SC "What is apparent is real". The onus to prove that the apparent is not real is on the party who claims it to be so. In this case it was the department which claimed that the amount of fixed deposit received belonged to the respondent firm even though the receipt had been issued in the name of another. It was held that the burden lies on the department to prove that the respondent was the owner of the amount despite the fact that the receipt was in the name of some other person.

3.24. The general rule is that apparent is to be taken as the real state of affairs unless contrary is proved. CIT vs Durga Prasad More 80 ITR 540 (SC).

3.25. Addition in block assessment to be covered under section 158B(b) must be based on concrete material. Sale price of car can not be increased merely on suspicion. Digvijay Chemicals Ltd vs ACIT 68 TTJ 280 (Del).

D. **Books of Accounts – Loose Papers**

3.26. Presumption of Section 132(4A) is applicable in assessment of search cases in respect of books of accounts and documents found in search Smt. Kesar Bai vs ITO 32 ITD1(Hyd) and Friends overseas (P) Ltd vs DCIT 73TTJ (Del)367.

3.27. Section 132(4A) can not be invoked for the purpose of regular asstt. It has limited application for order under section 132(5). If section 110 of Evidence Act is applied using these as evidence, then the presumption that it belongs to the assessee cannot be drawn as provided in section 132(4A). The presumption will in such case be that it belongs to the person whose name is stated on such document. Pushkar Narain Saraf vs CIT (1990)183 ITR 388(All).

3.28. Presumption under section 132(4A) in respect of any document or books of accounts found is restricted to the person from whose possession books of accounts or other documents were found and not against any other person. Further, presumption under section 132(4A) is a rebuttable presumption and not a conclusive one. Straptex India (P) Ltd vs DCIT 79 TTJ 228 (Mumbai)

3.29. Books of accounts — evidentiary value of diary—unilateral entry only. CBI vs V.C. Shukla 3 SCC 410-428.

3.30. Loose papers found during the search of assessee's premises on the letter pad of a third party with some noting in unidentified handwriting has no evidentiary value and no addition could be made solely on the basis of the said papers as the content of the document could not be linked or correlated with the assessee. Satnam Chhabra vs DCIT 74 TTJ 976

3.31. Addition on the basis of diary/loose sheets can not be made. S P Goyal vs Deputy CIT 77 TTJ 0001(TM) Bom.

3.32. The Hon'ble Delhi Tribunal in S.K. Gupta vs. DCIT 63 TTJ 532 has held that additions made merely on the basis of loose sheet and torn papers is not justified and the revenue has to bring some corroborative evidence to show that the loose papers and sheet actually show some transactions and that the assessee has earned income out of it, which is undisclosed from the department. It further held that the revenue can tax only those receipts which must have been proved to be income in the hands of the assessed/ recipient. Therefore, before assessing any receipt as taxable income, the onus is on the revenue to prove that the receipt of income of the assessee/ recipient and this can be proved or established only on the basis of some material or evidence.

3.33. Amount stated in the sale deed can not be ignored on the basis of agreement of sale unless it is proved that the agreement of sale was acted upon and the amount stated in the agreement was actually paid. On the basis of agreement to sell it can not be concluded that the price mentioned in the sale deed is not correct. CIT vs Smt. K.C. Agnes 128 Taxmann 848 (Kerala)

3.34. The Hon'ble Mumbai Tribunal in the case of M/s Vighnahar Builders & Developers Vs. ACIT, IT(S&S)A No.105/Mum/98, Bench-A Order dated 20-4-1999 has held that in the cases of search, the Assessing Officer has to bring some evidence or instance in order to make additions for sale of flats and shops at the rates adopted by the Stamp Authorities or the market rates prevailing at the time of Registration as compared to the rate of sale of flats and shops declared by the assessee as also disclosed in the Agreement for sale. It further held that the sound basis for making the addition would firstly be the date of booking for determining the price received by the assessee and not the date of registration and secondly, unless and until the actual receipts are found to be more than the agreed price, no addition can be made merely on the basis of surmises and conjectures in view of the decision of the Supreme Court in K.P. Varghese vs. ITO 131 ITR 597(SC).

3.35 In the course of search action certain materials were gathered by the department which disclosed omission or suppression of Sales only for certain periods of the Asstt.Year 1997-98. The department based on this material , estimated the undisclosed income of the assessee for the earlier years. The Tribunal held that the estimation of undisclosed income for the earlier years, on the basis of material for the later part period, is not warranted. The result of the year of search cannot be projected in to the past. The Tribunal relied on the decision the Hon'ble Supreme Court in Raghubar Manda vs. State of Bihar 8 STC 770 and the Hon'ble Orissa High Court in State of Orissa vs. Auto Electric Industries 83 STC 191 and J. Gopal Rao Vs. State of Orissa 88 STC 488. Relying on the aforesaid decisions, it held that the material located during search relates only to the year of search and as such it cannot be projected into the earlier years comprised in the Block Period. M/s Shadilal & Sons vs. ACIT, IT(S&S)A No.296/Mum/97,Bench-B order dt.25.9.1998.

E. **Statement/Retraction of Statement.**

3.36. Statements recorded at the time of search and later on contradicted even in the case of sale/purchase transaction are not conclusive and need to be ignored.

3.37. The Hon'ble Mumbai Tribunal in Mahaveer Traders Vs. Asstt. CIT IT(S&S)A. No.35/Mum/96, Bench-B Order dated 12.1.1999 has held that the department ought to have material or evidence or information or documents to support its claim that *on money* was charged by the assessee to treat the same as undisclosed income of the assessee. The Tribunal deleted the addition of the alleged *on money* received by the assessee as the said addition was made merely on the basis of the statement of the employees of the assessee which was retracted subsequently.

3.38. Confession was obtained on the basis of documents and papers for Rs. 8.5 lakhs, worked out by theA.O, which weren't produced before Tribunal/ assessee. Hence surrender based on misrepresenting the facts can't stand and was deleted. Baldev Krishan Kapoor v ACIT (2000) 245 ITR 102 AT(TM)

3.39. Addition simply on the basis of a statement or surrender of income can not be sustained.

(i) Nagubai Ammal v Sharma Rao (1956) AIR 1956 SC 593

(ii) Avadh Kishore Dass V Ram Gopal (1979) AIR 1979 SC 861

(iii) Sarwan Singh Rattan Singh v State of Punjab (1975) AIR 1957 SC 637

(iv) Shri Krishan v Kurukshetra University(1976) AIR 1976 SC 376

3.40. The assessee recorded the statement in the course of Survey declaring an income of Rs.4.00 Lakhs in the form of cash. Based on this admission alone and without any corroborated evidences, the A.O made an addition but CIT(Appeal) deleted the addition & Honourable Tribunal also upheld the order of CIT(A) on the ground that there was no evidence to indicate that the amount of Rs.4.00 lakhs constitute an income in the hands of the assessee. ACIT Vs Satya Narayan Aggarwalla 255 ITR AT 69 (Kol)

3.41. The assessee surrendered Rs.56.00 lakhs amount in his statement recorded under section 132(4) but later on retracted after going through the seized documents and offered only Rs. 37,96,395/- in the Return of Income. The A.O made the addition of Rs. 18,24,550/- being difference amount as recorded in the statement & return of income but was deleted on the plea that assessee made surrender without recourse to the seized material._Karan Chand v ACIT(2000) 73 ITD 434 (Chd).

3.42. "It is an established principal of law that a party is entitled to show and prove that the admissions made by him, is in fact, not correct and true." Nagindas Dahyabhai Patel v ACIT (1999) 104 Taxman 80(Ahd)

3.43. The assessee was in the business of lending money against the security of Gold/Silver and during survey operation out of 461 persons named, 91 persons name weren't correctly mentioned but loan given to them against Gold/.Silver were found to be correct and accepted by the department. However, A.O treated the Gold found against there borrowers as income of assessee under section 69 being acquired out of undeclared income. It was held that addition made by the A.O isn't sustainable on the ground that he cannot on the one hand accept the loan transaction as favourable to revenue & ignore the second part of pledged gold as to the property of borrower. Further it was also held the A.O has a limited power to make enquiries on oath under section 132(4) in respect of this findings from search & not authorized to put questions in general. ACIT v. Vasantlal Mehta (2001) 77 ITD 76 (Rajkot)

F. **Others**

3.44 When an assessee comes forward with an explanation that suppressed income as found by the A.O. is introduced in the cash book as cash credit it should be taken as reasonable explanation unless contrary is established by the A.O. CIT vs Shri Gudia Satyanarayana 1975 Tax LR 4 (AP).

3.45. In block assessment, the duty of the A.O. is to compute the undisclosed income for each assessment year separately as per the law applicable for that assessment year. There can not be consolidated income for the block period. Lakshmi Jewellers vs ACIT 73 TTJ 981 (Mad).

3.46. For action under Section 158BD, a satisfaction note from the Assessing Officer should be based on material. If the satisfaction note was contrary to material and evidence on record and the inference that certain parties did not exist was based on communication of enquiry officer and ignoring the other facts of the assessee, the notice under Section 158BD will be invalid and had to be quashed. Chhabria Marketing Ltd Vs DCIT (Mum) 81 ITD 314

3.47. Additional Director (Inv.) has no power to issue any authorization or warrant to Joint Director since the notification dated 6th September, 1989 issued by the Board authorized only the Director to exercise power under section 132(1). Dr. Nalini Mahajan vs Director of IT 122 Taxman 897 (Del)

3.48. Restraint order under section 132(3) does not amount to seizure. As such, where search is temporarily suspended by passing a restraint order, the search proceedings are not continued and limitation prescribed under section 158BC of 2 years is to be counted from the date of original panchnama. CIT vs Sandhya P Naik 124 Taxman 384 (Bom)

3.49. Initiation of search is when first step is taken toward search and the first step is taken when the search warrant is signed, not when the search warrant is executed. Nirmal Ghosh Bag vs DCIT 82 ITD 788 (Calcutta)

3.50. The Supreme Court in the case of Union of India vs Ajit Jain 260 ITR 80 (SC) has upheld the order of the Delhi High Court whereby a search carried out under section 132(1) was declared invalid on the ground that the same was based simply on information from the CBI. Such information can not be the basis for issue of warrant under section 132(1). For a valid search, information should provide reason for believing that the person concerned is in possession of money or other assets representing either wholly or in part income which has not been or which would not be disclosed by such person. Intimation simpliciter by the CBI that the money was found in the possession of the respondent which according to the CBI was undisclosed, without something more did not constitute information within the meaning of Section 132 of the Income Tax Act. Union of India vs Ajit Jain 260 ITR 80 (SC)

NO CONFESSIONAL STATEMENT IN THE COURSE OF SEARCH, SEIZURE AND SUREY

F.No. 286/2/2003 – IT (Inv)
GOVERNMENT OF INDIA
MINISTRY OF FINANCE & COMPANY AFFAIRS
DEPARTMENT OF REVENUE
CENTRAL BOARD OF DIRECT TAXES

Room No.254/North Block,
New Delhi, the 10th March, 2003

To

All Chief Commissioners of Income Tax, (Cadre Contra)
&
All Directors General of Income Tax Inc.,

Sir,

Subject : Confession of additional Income during the course of search & seizure and survey operation – regarding.

Instances have come to the notice of the Board where assesses have claimed that they have been forced to confess the undisclosed income during the course of the search & seizure and survey operations. Such confessions, if not based upon credible evidence, are later retracted by the concerned assesses while filing returns of income. In these circumstances, on confessions during the course of search & seizure and survey operations do not serve any useful purpose. It is, therefore, advised that there should be focus and concentration on collection of evidence of income which leads to information on what has not been disclosed or is not likely to be disclosed before the Income Tax Departments, Similarly, while recording statement during the course of search & seizures and survey operations no attempt should be made to obtain confession as to the undisclosed income. Any action on the contrary shall be viewed adversely.

Further, in respect of pending assessment proceedings also, assessing officers should rely upon the evidences/materials gathered during the course of search/survey operations or thereafter while framing the relevant assessment orders.

Yours faithfully,

Sd/-
(S.R. Mahapatra)
Under Secretary (Inv.II)